Ariel

little blue and little yellow

a story for Pippo and Ann
and other children
by Leo Lionni

an Astor Book

This is little blue.

Here he is at home with papa and mama blue.

Little blue has many friends

but his best friend is little yellow

who lives across the street.

How they love to play at *Hide-and-Seek*

and *Ring-a-Ring-O' Roses!*

In school they sit still in neat rows.

After school they run and jump.

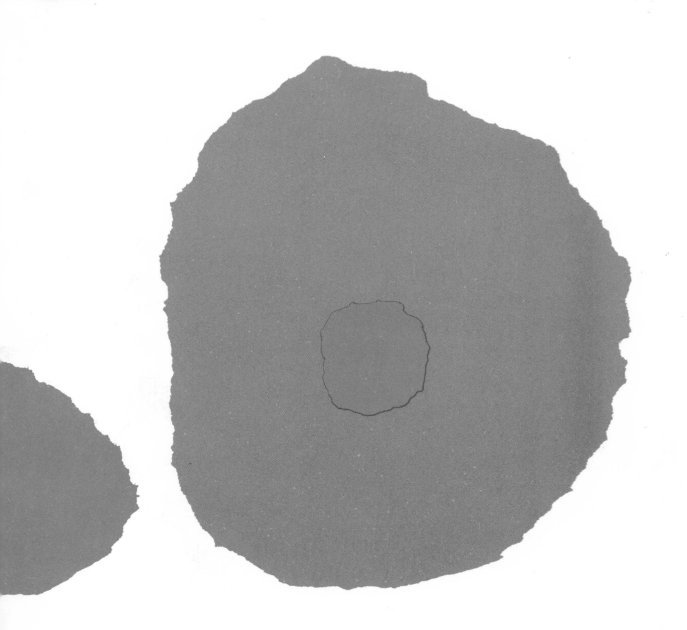

One day mama blue went shopping. "You stay home" she said to little blue.

But little blue went out to look for little yellow.

Alas! The house across the street was empty.

He looked here

and there

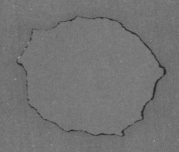

and everywhere...until suddenly, around ə corner

there was little yellow!

Happily they hugged each other

and hugged each other

until they were green.

Then they went to play in the park.

They ran through a tunnel.

They chased little orange.

They climbed a mountain.

When they were tired

27442   they went home.

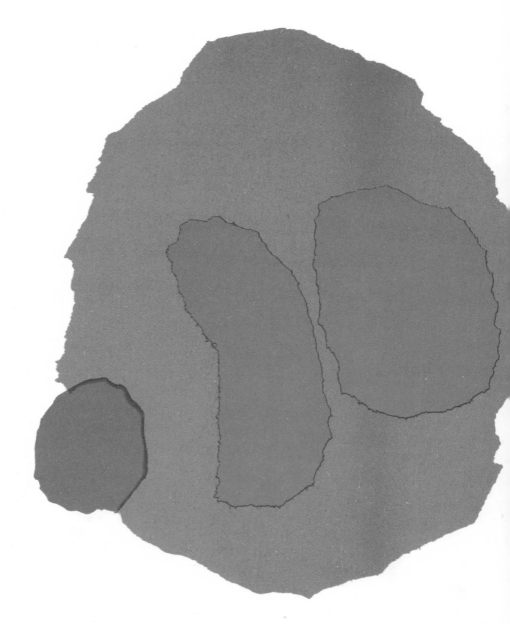

But papa and mama blue said: "You are not our little blue—you are green."

And papa and mama yellow said: "You are not our little yellow—you are green."

Little blue and little yellow were very sad. They cried big blue and yellow tears.

They cried and cried until they were *all* tears.

When they finally pulled themselves together they said: "Will they
believe us
now?"

Mama blue and papa blue were very happy to see their little blue.

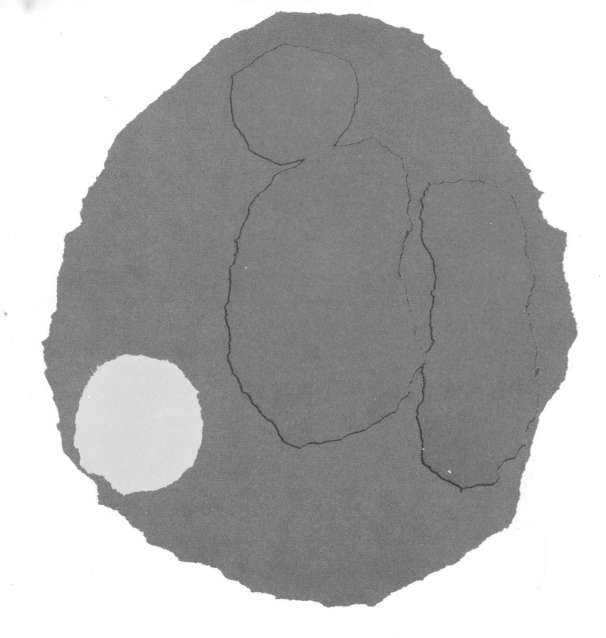

They hugged and kissed him

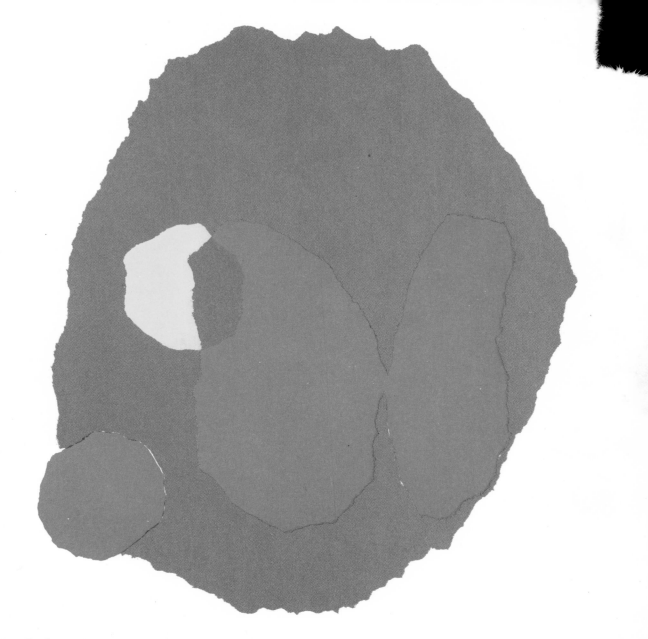

And they hugged little yellow too...but look . . . they became green!

Now they knew what had happened

and so they went across the street to bring the good news.

They all hugged each other with joy

and the children played until suppertime.

The End